Echo of the Star

illustrations and words
by CHRISTINE HILBERT

for

JONAH

the star was a great friend
to all of the creatures,
shining its light
for all to see.

As the night ended, the creatures grew sad to see the STAR leave.

"Morning is coming and I must go now,"

said the STAR.

"But don't be sad.

I will leave a bit of my SPARKLE so you

will always have a piece of me with you."

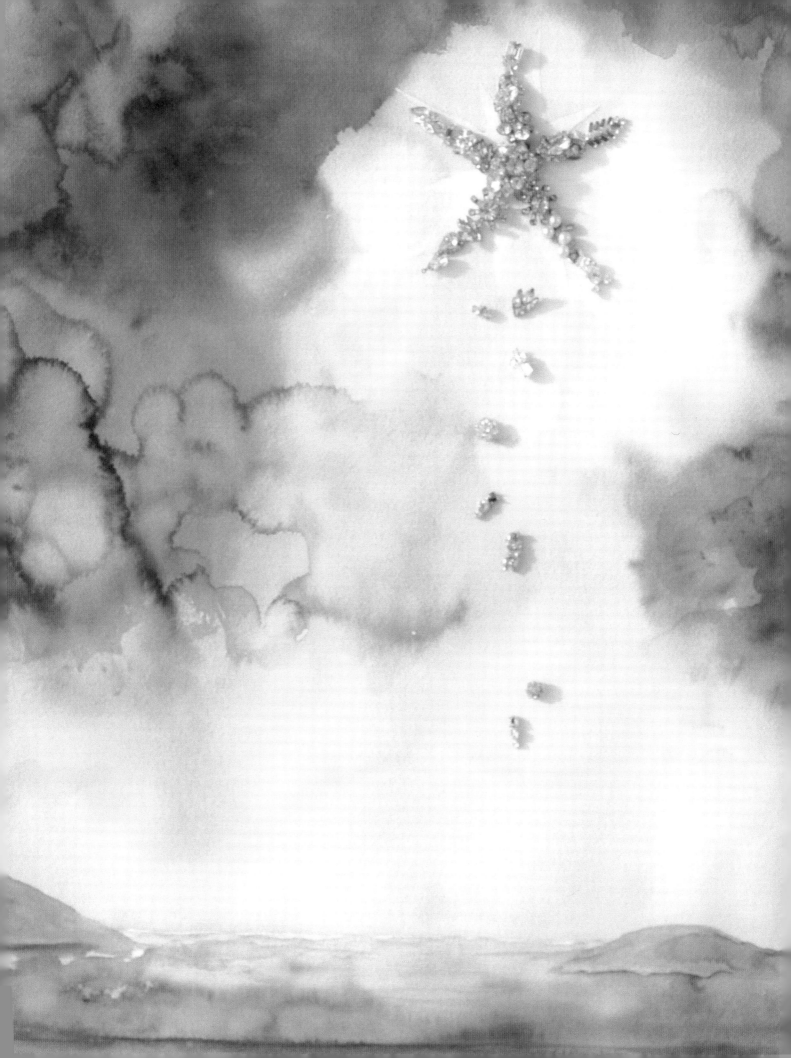

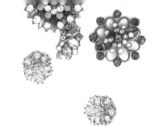

The W H A L E waved goodbye and

held tight to the S T A R 's S P A R K L E

It was happy.

The W H A L E sang a sweet song

for the S T A R as morning came.

A FLAMINGO heard the whale's song

and recognized the STAR 's

SPARKLE

on the WHALE.

It was happy.

The FLAMINGO

trumpeted the

sweet SPARKLE

to her friend

the CRAB.

The CRAB heard the trumpeting

and recognized the Star's SPARKLE

on the FLAMINGO.

It was happy.

The CRAB tip toed along to share the

sweet SPARKLE with the FLOWER.

The FLOWER heard the tip toeing and

recognized the STAR's SPARKLE on the CRAB.

It was happy.

The FLOWER whispered the

sweet

SPARKLED

song to his friend the BEE.

The BEE recognized

the STAR's SPARKLE on the flower.

It was happy.

The BEE buzzed off to share the

sweet SPARKLE with the OWL.

The OWL heard the BEE's buzzing

and recognized the STAR's SPARKLE.

It was happy.

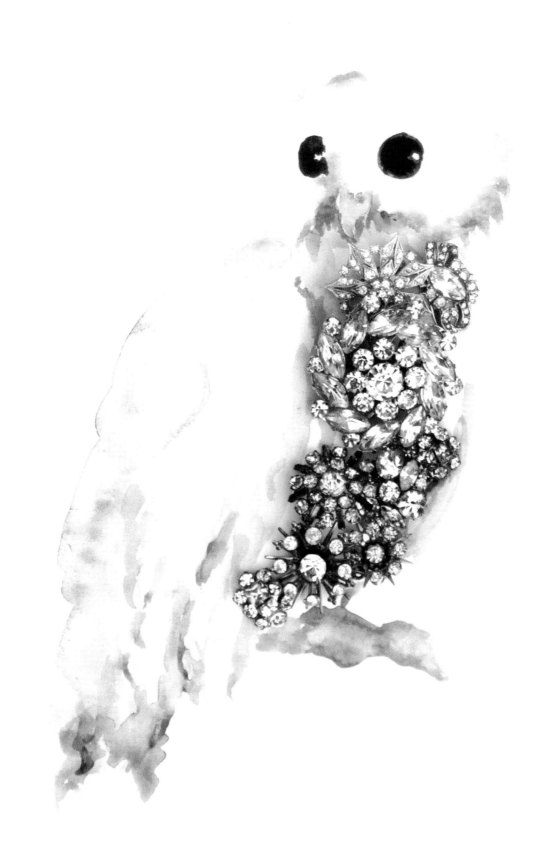

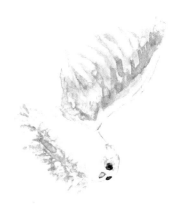

The OWL hooted the sweet SPARKLE

to her friend the RABBIT.

The RABBIT heard the OWL's hooting and

recognized the STAR's SPARKLE on the OWL.

It was happy.

The RABBIT ran off to share the

sweet SPARKLE with the CARDINAL.

The CARDINAL recognized the

STAR's SPARKLE on the RABBIT.

It was happy.

The CARDINAL was

overcome with love for the STAR.

It couldn't help but sing.

It still sings its sweet SPARKLED

song to remind us of the STAR's beauty,

even in the bright day.

When friends go away their love

SPARKLES within each one of us,

and when we shine our lights brightly

for one another we celebrate their love.